What Happened to the Pastors Family?

"LOST BUT FOUND"

ANITA RILEY

Published by Lee's Press and Publishing Company
www.LeesPress.net

Lee's
PRESS

A Premiere Self-Publishing
Services Company

ISBN-13: 979-8-9896434-9-3

PAPERBACK

Characters

Pastor: Mayceo

First Lady: Wife Lisa

Children: Terrence, Davesha, Marcus

Barbers: Lonnie, Tyrone

Deacons: Tom, Lee

Sisters: Tammy, Lawanda, Kim, Desha

Computer Man: Pete

Two Bad Guys

Cop

Scene One

Pastor and family are getting ready for church on a Sunday Morning.

Pastor Mayceo: Are you all ready yet? We're going to be late for church.

First Lady Lisa: No, I'm looking for my other shoe. Has anybody seen my shoe?

Davesha: No mom. You always lose your shoes... DADDY!! Terrence hid my belt, and I need it for my skirt.

Terrence: Girl, I don't have your belt! You better stay out of my face.

Pastor Mayceo: Terrence, that is no way to talk to your sister.

Terrence: You always take her side. It's like I don't matter. I *told* her I don't have her belt.

Pastor Mayceo: Ok, Terrence. Ok. Let's go. We're going to be late for church. We already missed half of Sunday school. Don't make me late for service. Let's go.

First Lady Lisa: Davesha and Marcus, come on. Your dad said let's go.

Marcus and Davesha: Okkkk mom.

(They leave for church)

Church Scene

They enter the church during praise and worship.

Pastor Mayceo: This is what I like to hear praising and worshiping the Lord.

First Lady Lisa: Whatever.

Pastor Mayceo: There you go already. You haven't gotten into the church good before you say something negative out your mouth.

Marcus: Mom and dad do you have to get into it at church again??

First Lady Lisa: No, baby I wasn't...

Pastor Mayceo: *(interrupts Lisa)* It's your mother, son.

First Lady Lisa: Let's go and sit down before I say something to you, Mr. Pastor *will* regret I said.

Pastor Mayceo: Lisa, please go take the children and sit down.

Pastor Mayceo enters the pulpit. Praise and worship have ended. He enters the podium.

Pastor Mayceo: Let's pray. Father God, I come to you in the name of Jesus asking Lord, that you anoint me afresh today. Give me your word for your people. Amen. Let the church say amen.

Church: Amen

Pastor Mayceo: We will be coming from 1 Corinthians. Chapter 2 verse 5 *(reads scripture twice)* why does the bible say that your faith must not stand in the wisdom of men, but in the power of God? Now that's saying something right there!

Deacon Tom: Preach Pastor Preach

Sister Lawanda: Deacon be quiet! We can't hear the pastor preach every Sunday for you yellin' "preach pastor preach" before he gets started.

Sister Kim: Lawanda, you need to shut up too! All you talk about is how fine the pastor is, and how you want him to get next to you.

Deacon Lee: Will all of you be quiet? We don't need this mess in God's house.

Sister Tammy: Deacon Lee who do you think you are talking to? My mother didn't tell me to be quiet and she is dead and gone now.

Deacon Tom: Yep, and that's why she is dead and gone now you talked her into her grave.

Terrence: I want to hear that in God's house because my dad and my mom are both hypocrites. I live with them, and I know. That's why I sit here and text my girlfriend while I'm in church. I'm going to tell them I'm going over to a buddy's house and going to see my girl. They won't know. They are all tied up in their separate lives they won't know a thing.

Sister Tammy: Terrence you're only 16 you don't need to start lying to your parents now. They love you.

Sister Dasha: Shh, shh, shh, we are still in church. *(Dasha jumps up)* OOHHH, I KNOW that's right. Thank you,

Jesus.

First Lady Lisa: Huh, we all need to preach to him.

Deacon Lee: What do you mean first lady?

First Lady Lisa: I know Pastor is seeing someone else.

Deacon Lee: Why you say that?

First Lady Lisa: I know my husband.

Deacon Lee: I really think the pastor is a good man and preacher and doer of the Word.

First Lady Lisa: Well, I *live* with your pastor. I know.

Deacon Lee: Ok, First Lady you live with him.

Pastor Mayceo: Amen Church. Church dismissed.

Scene Two

On the way home

Sister Lawanda: First Lady, are you coming over later on today?

First Lady Lisa: Yes, I'll be there. *(Turns to Pastor Mayceo)* Come on Pastor, I'm ready to go home.

Pastor Mayceo: Wait a minute, I'm talking.

First Lady Lisa: All you do is talk, let's go!

(Pastor looks at wife Lisa and shakes his head)

Pastor: Ok Deacon Tom, I'll see you on Wednesday.

Deacon Tom: Ok pastor be blessed.

(They walk off and go home)

(Pastor and family are at home preparing to eat dinner)

Pastor: Thanks for fixing dinner baby.

First Lady: You're welcome! O, later I'm going to sister Lawanda's house. It's a girl thing tonight.

Davesha: Mom, can I go? You always go over Sis. Lawanda's house.

First Lady: Girl be quiet while you still have lips. I will knock them off. And no, you can't go.

(Davesha looks at her dad.)

Pastor: Baby, we'll go out later.

Marcus: Can I go too, dad?

Pastor: Yes, Marcus you can. Terrence, do you want to go too?

Terrence: No dad, I was going to ask you and mom if I can go over to a friend's house.

(Lisa gets up from the table and leaves)

Pastor: Lisa, where you going?

Lisa: Didn't I tell you I was going over Lawanda's?

Pastor: But we haven't finished dinner yet.

Lisa: I gotta go. *(Putting on her coat)*

Pastor: Go ahead.

Terrence: So, can I go, dad?

Pastor: Yes, Terrence, yes.

(Terrence gets his coat and leaves too. Pastor, Davesha, and Marcus left sitting at the table.)

Davesha: Daddy, can we go to the movies?

Pastor: No, I need to run by the barbershop. Lonnie and Tyrone started opening on Sunday after church about 3 weeks ago. You stay here until I get back.

Marcus: Daddy, we want to go with you.

Davesha: Yea, daddy, can we go?

Pastor: No, I'll be back in about an hour or so. Lock the door and don't open it for anyone. Your mother and brother have keys and Davesha stay off that laptop.

Marcus and Davesha *(looking sad)*: Ok dad.

(Pastor leaves the room)

Davesha: Marcus, why are we always left at home? Mom, dad, and Terrence are never home. What is going on?

Marcus: All we can do is pray for them Davesha.

Davesha: Well, I'm going to get on my laptop and talk to my friends.

(They leave the room)

Scene Three

Lisa and Lawanda are meeting.

(There's a knock-on Lawanda's door)

Lawanda: Who is it?

Lisa: Lawanda it's Lisa.

(Lawanda opens the door.)

Lawanda: Come in, Hey girl! I miss all the things we used to do. Things have changed. Remember how we would go to the club and guys would try to hit on us. Girl, they didn't know we wanted the same thing they did. (They look at each other and laugh)

Lisa: Yes, girl I know, we had to cool things down. I remember how we used to look at those books too.

Lawanda: You right girl. Do you have any new books that we can look at?

Lisa: Yep, have them right here. Look girl, look at this.

Lawanda: OOO girl that looks good we should try that.

Lisa: Oh yes girl I think so too. *(They look at each other)* Girl I don't know how people call my husband a pastor. He is stupid, blind, and can't see. Don't that man know I'm with him for the money not for the kids and shoo' not for love. Girl, I spend all his money. Won't any other women get it? They may get something, but not his money.

Lawanda: I know that's right girl. I would keep him for a money bag too if I was you. Girl, what can he do? Can he do anything?

Lisa: Yea, he sits there like a knot on a log, talking about o baby, o baby. I say boy PLEASE will you hurry up. But look girl I got to go. I'll see you later this week, be ready.

(Lisa walks out the door)

Scene Four

Terrence is on the way to his girlfriend's house, but he never makes it. There are some guys on the corner shooting dice.

Guy 1: Preacher boy! What have you got in your pockets? Give it to us.

Guy 2: Yea, preacher boy.

(Terrence runs but the guys catches him, robs him, and beats him. He's on the corner all alone)

(Pastor at the barber shop)

Lonnie: Pastor? What's going on? Why you out and not home with your family on a Sunday?

Pastor: Man, sometimes I wish I wouldn't have gotten married. We're always fussing over the little things.

Tyrone: Pastor, I know. My wife and I go through the same thing. The kids see us fuss all the time and sometimes I just want out.

Lonnie: I'm glad no one tricked me into getting married. I was smart. Ya'll some dumb brothers. Even you pastor. I saw you with one of the women at church.

Pastor: No, it's not what you think.

Lonnie: Whatever, I know. Well, just watch yourself, pastor. It's some crazy women out here and you should know that you married one.

(They laugh)

Pastor: I gotta go. *(He leaves the shop)*

Tyrone: Pastor and his wife are playing with fire. God is not pleased with what is going on.

Lonnie: Man, Tyrone we just need to keep them up in prayer and not talk about them. *They leave the shop.*

(Pastor Mayceo knocks on Sister Lawanda's door. She opens the door.)

Lawanda: Hey baby you looked good at church today.

Pastor: You did too. I missed you and wanted to just grab you in church and just um um um, I shall not say.

Lawanda: When are you leaving your wife? You said we were going to grow old together. What is going on?

Pastor: Just give me some time.

Lawanda: You said that a year ago.

Pastor: Be patient. Baby be patient.

Lawanda: I'll wait because I love you. But when you are not here, I miss you and your touch, but I'll see what you going to do.

Pastor: Well baby, I gotta go. I left the kids home by themselves, so I got to leave now. I'll be back later, and we can bump and grind.

Lawanda: But you just got here.

Pastor: I'll make it up to you I promise.

Lawanda: Ok. See you later baby.

(Pastor puts on his coat. His phone rings, it's Lisa. On the phone Lisa tells the pastor that their son has been beaten

on the corner)

Lisa: Terrence has been hurt.

Pastor: Where is he?!

Lisa: On the corner of Prayer and Faith.

Pastor: I'll be right there. (Looks to Lawanda) Lawanda, Terrence is hurt; I have to go right now.

Lawanda: Can I go?

Pastor: NO! How would that look? No, you stay here. I'll call you as soon as I can. (He leaves. Lisa phone rings)

Lawanda: Hey baby.

Lisa: Terrence has been hurt.

Lawanda: What? Where is he?

Lisa: On the corner of Prayer and Faith.

Lawanda: Ok, baby. I'll be right there.

(Pastor and Lawanda arrive at the same time. They look at each other but don't say anything.)

Pastor: Terrence, Terrence!! Can you hear me? Who did this?!! Who did this?!!

Terrence: Nobody dad, nobody.

Lisa: You have to tell us.

Terrence: I don't know. Can we just go home?

Lawanda: Baby, you need to tell your father and mother what happened.

Terrence: I told you I don't know. *(They help him up and* *they all go home)*

(Back at the pastor's house)

Terrence: I'm going to get cleaned up.

Pastor: Why won't that boy talk to us?

Lisa: Maybe because you're never home.

Pastor: Shut your mouth! You are just as guilty as I am. You be running the streets with your friends all the time.

Lawanda: Don't start blaming each other for what happened. We need to keep God in this situation and let Him work it out.

Pastor: Yes, Sister Lawanda you're right. I'm going to call Terrence down here and maybe we can talk. *(Yells)* Terrence come down here!

Lawanda: See you later First lady and Pastor Mayceo. *(Sister Lawanda leaves)*

Terrence: Yes, dad?

Pastor: What is going on with you? Why won't you talk to your mother and me?

Terrence: I told you dad, nothing.

Pastor: Ok. Since you won't talk to us, you are grounded. No car, no going to the games at school, no company and give me your cell phone, until you want to talk.

Terrence: Whatever. (He gives his dad the keys to the car and cell phone. He walks back up the stairs. Pastor and Lisa stand there looking at each other.)

Lisa: Well, so called Pastor, what you going to do now?

You trying to keep people in church in line you can't even keep your family in line.

Pastor: Will you please be quiet.

Lisa: Whatever.

Pastor: I'm going to the barbershop.

Lisa: For what?

Pastor: I need to talk to some of the guys.

Lisa: What?! Talk to me. I'm your wife, that's our son.

(Pastor leaves for the barbershop. Lisa calls Sister Tammy)

Tammy: Hello.

Lisa: Hey Tammy, are you busy? I need to talk to you about the kids and pastor.

Tammy: First lady, I'm busy now. Maybe we can talk later.

Lisa: Ok, talk to you later.

(Lisa calls Sister Kim)

Lisa: Hello Kim? Are you busy? I really need a friend to talk to.

Kim: No, I'm not busy. I'll be right over. (She hangs up and goes to the pastor's house. She arrives and Lisa lets her in.)

Kim: Hey girl, what's up?

Lisa: We are having problems here. The whole family is jacked up. Pastor is doing whatever, the kids are out of control, and I'm doing my own thing. I just don't want to be married or have a family anymore.

(Kim's phone rings)

Kim: Hello. Ok, honey. (Hangs up phone) First lady, I got to go my boyfriend is coming over.

Lisa: You just got here.

Kim: And now I've just got to leave. Bye, girl. You better work this out with the pastor. *(Kim leaves. Lisa calls sister Dasha)*

Dasha: Hello.

Lisa: Hey girl this is Lisa. Can you come over?

Dasha: No first lady, but we can talk over the phone. What's up?

Lisa: Well pastor and I are having problems in our marriage.

(Dasha cut her off)

Dasha: Bye girl I got to go. You better talk to God. (She hangs up)

Lisa: Terrence, Marcus, Davesha! I'm going out for a minute. Stay in the house until I get back.

Terrence: I'm not a babysitter.

Marcus: I don't need a babysitter. I babysit you, Terrence.

Terrence: Boy be quiet before I slap you.

Marcus: You are not going to touch me. I'll put God on you.

Davesha: Mom, can I go with you?

Lisa: No stay here with your brother. They need someone

to babysit them.

Davesha: Ok mom. Ya'll hear mom, I'm in charge.

Terrence and Marcus: Whatever. *(Lisa leaves. The kids sit down and start talking)*

Davesha: Mom and dad are never here; we are raising ourselves. Terrence and Marcus, I got a secret I want to tell you. I have a friend that I talk to on the Internet he says his name is Pete. He is nice to me, he said he will give me all the things I can't get at home.

Marcus: Davesha you better leave that man alone. That is not right; you know at night I pray to God that He brings our family together again.

Terrence: That's all you talk about is God. If God wanted this family together God wouldn't have messed it up. God got dad running here and there and mom needs him. Mom is just out there, and she don't know what to do. Davesha, if you have a friend, you better talk to mom about it. You are only 13. Well, if dad and mom split up, I'm going with dad.

Davesha: Don't talk about mom and dad splitting up. I want them to stay together. Anyway, Terrence God didn't mess this family up, mom and dad did, and my friend doesn't have anything to do with this family I think he loves me.

Terrence: Whatever. Come on guys let's go play the game.

Davesha: You go play the game. I'm going to talk to my friend.

Davesha: *(at her laptop)* Pete are you on.

Pete: Yes, baby girl I'm on. I have been waiting for you. I want to see you. The picture you sent me doesn't show the real you, I know you are a beautiful young lady, and I would love to meet you.

Davesha: Well, I'm only 16 and my mother won't let me come out at night.

Pete: What time can you come out? I will make my time your time baby. I love you.

Davesha: After school about 3:30.

Pete: I can't meet you at the school but what about around the corner at the store?

Davesha: Ok, I guess I can, but I got to be back home by 6:30. I'll tell my brother to tell my mother I'm at the library.

Pete: Ok, baby. I'll see you at 3:30. Can't wait to see you.

Davesha: Can't wait to see you too.

Pete: I love you, Baby. I'm going to make you so happy and make you feel so good. Would you like that baby?

Davesha: Yes, yes, I would like that can I see you now?

Pete: You want to see me now? What about your mother and father?

Davesha: They are not home.

Pete: What time will they be home?

Davesha: Late tonight, please can I see you?

Pete: Yes, baby you can. Where do you live?

Davesha: 777 Jesus Way

Pete: That's great. I live a few blocks from you. I can be there in 20 min. See you soon. Be ready. I'll meet you outside on the next block over from your house.

Davesha: Ok. *(Davesha goes to put on her coat in leaves the house)*

(Pastor at the barbershop)

Pastor: Hey guys what's up? Man, I need a guys' input on something.

Lonnie: Man, you don't need *our* input, you need Jesus.

Tyrone: Man, that's all you talk about is Jesus, Jesus, Jesus.

Lonnie: Yep, if you knew what I've been through, you would believe in Him too.

Tyrone: Man, we know about that accident, and how you almost died. So what?

Lonnie: I saw Jesus on the cross that night on that hospital bed. He said because of the strife I have taken for you, you shall live.

Pastor: What? You mean to tell me that you saw Jesus and he spoke with you?

Lonnie: Yes, man; Pastor that's when I changed my life completely.

Pastor: Well, maybe you can help me figure out some problems I'm having at home with my family.

Lonnie: Pastor, you need to pray and seek Jesus.

Pastor: You think like everyone else. You think because I'm a pastor I don't need guidance. All I need is a friend to talk to, someone I can trust.

Tyrone: Pastor, you can trust me.

Pastor: Tyrone, I can trust you as far as I can see you.

(Tyrone laughs)

Tyrone: I know I talk too much, but I *can* keep a secret.

Lonnie: Pastor, what is it?

Pastor: I am seeing another woman.

Lonnie and Tyrone: NO, pastor! Not you?!

Pastor: Yea, it's me. I didn't want it to happen it just did.

Lonnie: Pastor, we need to pray for God to guide you. And you already know what you need to do.

Tyrone: Pastor, what are you going to do? I'll tell you what I'd do. I'd keep lady one at home and lady two in the street. I'll have my cake and eat it too.

Pastor: I need to go pray and seek God. *(They leave the stage)*

(Davesha and Pete Meet)

Pete: Hello, are you Davesha?

Davesha: Yes, are you Pete?

Pete: Yes baby, I'm Pete. You are lovely. Come on let's go before someone see us, ok? I'm not going to hurt you, baby. I only want to love you.

Davesha: Ok, but you promise you will have me home before my mother and father get home.

Pete: Yes, baby I will. Come on now let's go.

Davesha: ok. *(she leaves with Pete)*

Lawanda: *(talking to God)* God, if you can hear me, please answer me. I know what I'm doing is wrong, but when I try to do good evil is always present. Lord my life is a mess. Please, Lord Fix it. You see, Lord, I do what I do because of money. I work every day Lord and still can't make ends meet. So, I playhouse with the pastor and the pastor's wife. I'm tied Lord. Please help me.

Lisa knocks at Lawanda's door.

(Lisa is over sister Lawanda's house. Lisa walks in)

Lisa: Hey baby. I had to come see you. I love you and wish we could be together.

Lawanda: I know baby just wait, we will. I have a plan to get the pastor out of the way.

Lisa: What is the plan?

Lawanda: You'll see soon enough.

Lisa: Pastor doesn't do anything for me anymore. If I would have known this, I wouldn't have gotten married. Our life is a mess. *(They hug)*

Lawanda: It's okay. *(There is a knock on the door)* Who could that be?

Lisa: This is your house. I don't know.

Lawanda: Who is it?

Pastor: It's me baby. Open up.

Lisa: Is that my husband?

Pastor: I need to talk with you.

Lawanda: Come in.

Pastor: Lisa! What are you doing here?

Lisa: What are YOU doing here? And what do you mean, "Baby, it's me open up"?

Pastor: I'm in love with her.

Lisa: Well, Lawanda and I have been seeing each other for over a year.

Pastor: What? We've been seeing each other for two years now, and you two have been seeing each other too?

Lisa: No, this can't be true.

Lawanda: Yes, it is. I have been seeing the both of you. First lady, I had something that you weren't getting at home and the same goes for you pastor. He needed me; you were always nagging and complaining. See, all I had to be is what the both of you wanted. And I got what I wanted money, clothes, cars, and a house. So, I just played your game. Now, the both of you get out of my house.

(Pastor and first lady look at each other and they both leave to go home. They arrive home)

Pastor: Lisa, you know things have not been right between us for a long time now. And after tonight, I can't do this anymore. You see, I'm in love with Lawanda, and I was going to leave you for her. But after tonight, I'm going to step down as pastor, and I need some time away from this marriage. I need to do some soul searching with God.

Lisa: That was Lawanda's plan, get you to herself. Well, she can have you! And I agree, we need to separate so I can get my life together. I never believed in you anyway. I was there for the security. Now, that I have these kids I have all the security I need.

Pastor: So, we both agree to separate? Even if it leads to divorce, I'm ready.

Lisa: Yes.

(Pastor calls the kids into the room)

Pastor: Sit down. We have something we need to talk to you about.

Terrence: What now?

Marcus: I'm sleepy, can we talk tomorrow?

Lisa: Where is Davesha?

Terrence: She was in her room on her laptop the last time I saw her.

Pastor: Davesha come down here now! *(They wait for an answer from Davesha no answer, they all run to her room.)*

Marcus: She is not here. Where could she be?

Terrence: Dad, Davesha said she had a friend on the net that she was talking to. Look at her laptop.

Pastor: Where is her laptop? (They look for it but cannot find it)

Lisa: O My God where is my baby? Call the police.

(They call the police ring, ring no answer at the station.)

Pastor: No answer let's go look for her. *(They all put their coats on in go look for Davesha, no one has seen her or heard from her, so they go to the police station.)*

Pastor: My daughter is MISSING

Police: Pastor, I know you are worried, but we will look for her give us a description of what she had on.

Lisa: I don't know.

Pastor: I don't know. Terrence, Marcus do you know what your sister had on?

Terrence: Nope I don't dad.

Marcus: No dad *(Marcus crying)* Where is Davesha?

Police: We will do what we can to find her.

Pastor: Come on boys we need to talk in look for your sister.

Lisa: Terrence. Marcus. I know what we have to tell you is going to hurt, and I know you are already hurting because we don't know where your sister is. But A lot of families go through this, so you will get over it.

Terrence: What is it?

Lisa: Your dad and I are separating. But we are going to stay together until we find your sister.

Marcus: No, No! I don't want this! I've prayed every night for God to bring this family closer.

Terrence: Dad, you never stand up to mom. You *always* let her do and say what she wants. Why does our family need to separate? And now that Davesha is missing, what are we going to do? That's my sister!

(Marcus gets up and hugs his dad, crying)

Pastor: We are going to do all we can to find your sister.

And Marcus, son, we both agreed to separate.

Terrence: Where are we going to go?

Lisa: With me.

Terrence: No mom, I'm going with dad.

Marcus: I'm staying with mom.

Pastor: That's fine. We are not fussing tonight; let's all try to think of where Davesha would go. *(They leave the stage)*

Church Scen

(Tom, Lee, and Dasha singing "Come by Here")

Kim: Where is Lawanda? She is never late.

Tammy: Giiiirl, you don't know? She was doing both of them. *And* Davesha is missing.

Kim: What? Girl, what are you talking about?

Tammy: Nothing, girl, nothing. You'll see in church today.

(Tom, Lee, and Dasha sit down. Pastor Mayceo walks in)

Pastor: Good morning, church. I have something to say this morning. My family has some personal problems; my daughter is missing. She was talking to a man online and now; we can't find her. I need to step down from pastoring this church. I'm sure you'll find someone else who can lead God's people. I need to seek God for myself and my family. I need to pray we find our daughter.

Tom: Pastor! Pastor! *(Pastor turns and walks off the church grounds. The church falls silent)*

Tammy: *(crying)* This is my home church. Now what am I going to do? We've got to do something to help the first lady and pastor find Davesha.

Kim: That's why we need to know the Word for ourselves, so when something like *this* happens, we won't be lost. We'll look for her.

Deacon Tom: We better seek God for another pastor, and pray God helps them find their daughter.

Deacon Lee: Sisters let's get together Wednesday for bible study and come up with a plan to get another pastor. I pray that God helps them find their daughter.

Tammy: Wait, wait. We need to wait and see if the Pastor will change his mind.

Deacon Lee: Did you read his face? He's not coming back.

Deacon Tom: I'll see you at bible study.

(They all leave)

Pastor (on stage): Dear Lord, I need your guidance right now. Lord, help me find my daughter. It is not about my family just me this time. I need help. I'm crying out to you. *(Singing)*

What Happened to the Pastors Family?

PART 2

Characters

Pastor: Mayceo

First Lady: Lisa

Dr. Sue: A lady's voice

Lawyer: No character

Children: Terrence, Davesha, Marcus

Pastor: Jenkins

Pastor: Smith

Two Bad Guys: No characters

Mr. Concord: Character

Computer Man Pete wife Linda

Sisters: Tammy, Lawanda, Lawan Lawanda's son, Kim, Desha

Deacons: Lee, Tom: Police two

Barbers Shop: Lonnie, Tyrone

Song Marvin Gay: Let's stay together.

Scene One

Counseling Session

(Pastor at a counseling session: sitting at the table talking with Pastor Jenkins and Pastor Smith.)

Pastor Jenkins: What's going on Pastor Mayceo? I hear your family is *destroyed*. Do you want to talk about it?

Pastor Smith: Maaaannn, don't be like me. I waited too long and lost everything I had. Divorce is not a good thing for any family. Pastor Mayceo, what is really going on?

Pastor Mayceo: I messed up man. I messed up. I find myself asking why I did it. How could I have let my wife and children down? They believed in me. I let the church down. My daughter is missing. I don't know whether she is dead or alive. The police keep saying, "We are looking for her." But it's been 6 months and nothing yet. God, what I'm I going to do?

Pastor Jenkins: First of all, you've got to *totally* submit to God. Then you gotta get down on your knees and pray, man. Pray. God wants all of you not 99.5.

Pastor Smith: Jenkins, be quiet! All I hear you say is pray, pray, pray. Well, I prayed too. I prayed until I was blue in the face. I almost died on my knees praying so hard. My family still left me. I was so mad with God I kicked a steel pole and broke my toe. *That* hurt but not as bad as losing my family. (They all laugh.)

Pastor Jenkins: You deserve what *you* got. Telling your wife, you have a woman in every state? What was wrong with you man? You must have been crazy! I would have left you too; did you have a baby in each state too?

Pastor Mayceo: Man, this is supposed to be about *me* and what *I* need to do.

Pastor Smith: I can't tell you nothing! I'm just in as bad shape as you. I don't even have a home. (He cries).

Pastor Jenkins: (Jumps up from the table.) Smith, be quiet and stop acting like a wimp! *Mr. Woman in each state.*

Pastor Mayceo: Man, y'all can't help me? I'm out of here, I need some counseling. He shakes his head and leaves.

Pastor Smith: Jenkins, we got to help him in some kind of way. I know how he feels. It's not a day that goes by that I don't think about getting my family back. But only God can do that. Jenkins, I'm headed to the Barbershop.

(They both leave.)

Scene 2: First Lady Lisa goes over to sister Lawanda's house. (Knock at the door.)

Sis. Lawanda: Who is it?

First Lady Lisa: First Lady Lisa.

Sis. Lawanda: What she want? I haven't heard from her since I broke their marriage up. That showwwww wasssssss some gooddd money. I had all of it from both sides. I had my thing going on. But let me stop reminiscing, let me get to this door before she leaves. Let's see what she is talking about.

Sis. Lawanda opens the door and first lady walks in. They sit down.

Sis. Lawanda: What did I do to deserve this visit? I haven't seen you in six months. What did I do now?

First Lady Lisa: Nothing, I just wanted to come by and make my peace with you. I can't get to heaven hating no one.

Sis. Lawanda: You got that right.

First Lady Lisa: I forgive you and myself. I want to know if we can be friends. Not the way we once were but just casual friends, not messing around or under cover.

Sis. Lawanda: Are you sure you can be my friend? After all, got all this. *(Sis. Lawanda gets up and prances around the first chair.)*

First Lady Lisa: I have been in a Christian Center that has taught me the *right* way to live and conduct my newfound religion. It is a wonderful life.

Sis. Lawanda: What? I thought I could get you back under my wings, but I guess not.

First Lady Lisa: No, God came and did a work in me. I'm totally delivered from any kind of same sex anything. Honey, I can stand here and look at your body all day and don't even want to touch you at all. Thank you, Jesus. You see you got to want to be delivered.

Sis. Lawanda: Well, I guess I'm not delivered from that, yet. I still love it all. If you know what I mean?!!

First Lady Lisa: I once was like that, but I got serious with God, and God got serious with me. I know it may be hard to do, but put your trust in God, and he will make a change in you.

Sis. Lawanda: I don't believe God can do anything with me. See, I was dating another married man before your husband. I had a son from him, and he doesn't even know it. I've been hiding this life for nine years.

First Lady Lisa: What? The baby is nine years old? I never knew you had a son.

Sis. Lawanda: I know. Whenever you would come over, I would send him to my mother's house and keep his room door locked so no one could go in there.

First Lady Lisa: You are always hiding something. Where is he? Is he here?

Sis. Lawanda: Yes, Lawan come here baby, come here.

Lawan: Yes, mommy?

Sis. Lawanda: Here is my son.

First Lady Lisa: What? Is he from a Caucasian? Girl, you be doing Chinese, Japanese, Hispanic and Puerto Rican? Is there anything you don't do?

Sis. Lawanda: Yes, he is. That's why I have been hiding him, because if his dad finds out he will surely come and take him from me. He has his own law firm with 25 lawyers working for him. I can't take that chance of losing my son. He is all I have.

Lawan: Mommy, why are you crying? It's going to be ok.

First Lady Lisa: Sis. Lawanda, you got to give it all to God. He can and will fix it where you and your son won't ever want for anything. Just take it to God.

Sis. Lawanda: I can't, I've done too many wrong things in my life.

First Lady Lisa: Come with me to one of the meetings this week. Just sit and listen first then speak if you feel like it. Some of the ladies at the church go there too, we support each other. Come on, you will like it.

Sis. Lawanda: Girl the way I look and dress they may kick me out before I get into the door.

First Lady Lisa: Come on, say yes.

Sis Lawanda: I'll think about it.

First Lady Lisa: Say yes.

Sis. Lawanda: Ok, yes, newfound friend in Christ. Yes, but what will I do with Lawan? I can't keep taking him to my mom's house. She's always talking about how old she is getting, and how she can keep babysitting a rich man's kid and she ain't getting paid. First Lady, my mom and money! It's crazy and, she doesn't need it.

First Lady Lisa: Bring him to my house with my boys, you can't hide him forever.

Sis. Lawanda: Call me for the next meeting.

First Lady Lisa: I will. Don't be lying to me girl and saying you going to come and don't.

Sis. Lawanda: I'm coming. I gotcha. I'm coming.

First Lady Lisa: Okay, girl bye. (They leave the house.)

Scene Three

Meeting in the Church

Church Scene: Church members walking up to the pulpit.

Deacon: Tom and Lee looking at the women as they come up to the pulpit shaking their heads, eyes big about to pop out their heads.

Sis. Tammy: Deacon Lee and Deacon Tom what y'all looking at" Y'all fresh old men, I'll give you something to look at. (She shakes her butt at them and goes to sit down.) How you like me now? I know I got it going on.

Sis. Kim: Sis. Tammy, you need to stop acting up in God's house.

Sis. Dasha: Come on y'all we got to be serious, we come here Sunday after Sunday and sit in this church and pray that God sends us a pastor, but he hasn't yet, and it's been six months.

Deacon: Tom: So, you don't think I'm doing a good job at taking the pastor's place?

Deacon Lee: (Jumps up.) Say whattttt? You almost made me curse! Hell Heavens no! We need a pastor or our pastor back.

Deacon: Tom: Let's Pray.

Sis. Tammy: Every Sunday all we do is pray when we going to hear a word from God. Some pastor, you are Deacon Tom.

Deacon Tom: I'm not a pastor. I'm a deacon. I don't know how to preach. But I sure know how to look at the pretty women. I love me some women. I may be old, but I still got my eyes. *(He blinks his eyes.)*

Sis Dasha: We need to get us a pastor quick before we have a hoe house for a church. Deacon Tom and Deacon Lee, I see y'all up there talking to each other about the women that come in this church. But y'all saved huh?

Sis. Tammy: Where is the AC? It's hot in this building.

Deacon Tom: It's going to be hotter than this where you are going.

Sis. Tammy: Deacon Tom, you are pushing my patience.

Sis. Kim: Look, I think we need to close the church down until we find a pastor.

Sis. Tammy: Oh, no! You ain't closing my church down. Pastor, First Lady and Sis Lawanda may be gone but I'm not letting nobody close my church down. I'll come and stay in front of the building with all my ghetto Christian people. We'll fight-fight to keep this church open.

Sis. Kim: Let's just go home. I've had enough of church today.

Deacon Lee: We not going to pray out?

Deacon Tom. We've done enough praying today. Come on, Deacon Lee. *(He grabs deacon Lee by the arm and pulls him out of church. They all leave.)*

Scene Four

Davesha and Pete

Davesha: Where are you taking me now? It's been six months and I want to go home.

Pete: We're going to my house. I have a surprise for you there.

Davesha: I don't want to go to your house, I want to go home.

Pete: You are never going back to that place; they didn't treat you right. We are going to treat you really good. I have someone I want you to meet.

Davesha: What or who is it?

Pete: You'll love her. I was never going to hurt you.

They arrive at Pete's house. A woman comes out.

Davesha: Please let me go home. I've been with him for six months. My family is looking for me.

Wife: Did he hurt you or did he do anything to you?

Davesha: No, ma'am. I just want to go home.

Wife: You are my lovely daughter; your parents didn't treat you right now. It's my chance to show you how a young lady should be treated.

Davesha: No, can I please go home?

Pete: No, you are our daughter now. We've been watching you since you were about five. We saw how your parents treated you. They were never home, left y'all by yourselves all the time. Now, you have a family that loves you. Honey, show Davesha all the things we picked up for her. The wife picks up the clothes, shoes and jewelry and shows them to Davesha.

Davesha: All this for me, my parents never bought me stuff like this. Can I go try them on?

Wife: Yes, please do. Keep one of them on, we're going to go out to dinner later.

Davesha: All this is nice, but I still want to go home. I love my family.

Wife: Pete, can you do something to change her mind? She is a lovely young lady, and I would love to have her for our daughter.

Pete: *(Turns and talks to Davesha)* I know it was wrong how I got you to come with me, but that is the only way we know. But look if you stay, we will treat you very well. You will have anything you want. I know you're only 13, but we will get you a car, cell phone and whatever else you want, just name it you got it, just stay here with my wife and I. We just want you to be our daughter.

Davesha: I know it was wrong of me to talk to you like I did on the computer. I'm sorry please let me go home. It's been 6 months now and my parents probably think I'm dead. Please can I go home? It's been fun here. You gave me everything I've wanted but I want to go home please. *(She starts crying)*

Wife: Baby don't cry. I'll talk to Pete tonight, and we will give you an answer in the morning.

Davesha: Okay, goodnight. (They leave to go to bed.)

Scene Five

Two bad guys walking down the street see Pastor Smith.

Pastor Smith: Hello fellows, what y'all doing out this time of night?

Bad guy 1: We couldn't sleep, so we decided to take a walk.

Pastor Smith: Well, it's late, you need to be getting home.

Bad guy 2: Yes sir.

Pastor Smith: Wait a minute, can you help me with something? It will only take a minute.

Bad Guys look at each other.

Bad guys: Well, I guess we can. What is it?

Pastor Smith: Can you help me bring something to the church?

Bad guy 1: We ain't going in no church.

Bad guy 2: What? Why not?

Bad guy 1: *(Whispers in bad guy 2's ear)* You know what we did. We robbed a preacher's boy. Man, we go in that church God may light fire to us, and I'm not ready to burn yet.

Pastor Smith: Can you help me guys?

Bad Guys: We guess so. What we need to do?

Pastor Smith: I have a cross in my car that's too heavy for me to lift. Can you guys bring it in?

Bad guy number 2: Is that all it is? Man, we got this.

Bad guy 1: Man, I can't lift nothing, my back hurts. *(He limps around)*

Bad Guy 2: Man, come on. You wanted to do it at first, come on man.

Bad Guy 1: Ok, but if my back cracks you gonna put it back in place. (He limps off stage. They all leave.)

Scene Six

Lonnie and Tyrone see Pastor Smith coming to the barbershop.

Lonnie: Man, Tyrone we better lock our door. Here comes Pastor Smith all we going to hear about is how he lost his family. Man, that is old news everybody knows how he lost his family.

Pastor Smith: *(Enters the barbershop)* What's up fellas?

Tyrone: Hello, Pastor.

Lonnie: What's up man?

Tyrone: Man, you don't address a pastor as "what's up man."

Lonnie: Why not? He acts like one of us.

Tyrone: Man, it's called respect.

Lonnie: *(Walks over to the pastor smith)* Is it ok if I call you man?

Pastor Smith: You're the first person who ever asked me that. It doesn't matter. Call me what you want just not anything that doesn't line up with the word of God.

Lonnie: Alright.

Tyrone: Have y'all heard from Pastor Mayceo, it's been six months.

Pastor Smith: Yes, Pastor Jenkins and I talked with him today. He's good.

Lonnie: Is he back with his family?

Pastor Smith: No, his daughter is still missing too!

Lonnie: Whattt no way. Tyrone man we got to pray.

(Here comes Pastor Mayceo into the barber shop.)

Pastor Smith: Pastor, you following me?

Pastor Mayceo: No, I came to get a haircut. Don't I need one? *(He sits in Tyrone's chair)*

Lonnie: You look like a wolf. What happened? You haven't cut your hair since your family left?

Tyrone: Oh man you funny, you got jokes. Tyrone turns and looks at Pastor Mayceo. I'm sorry man sometimes Lonnie don't know what to say out his mouth.

Pastor Mayceo: It's cool it's cool, I need someone I can talk to, to help me get my life in order. I want my family, and I want my church back. If God can fix me, I want to be fixed. I want God to use me like never before. I've learned a very valuable lesson. Don't play with fire if you can't stand the heat. *(They laugh)*

Pastor Mayceo: Don't laugh, it could be you. I haven't talked to my wife or kids since we split up. I want to call her man. I miss her. Y'all may think I'm a wimp, but I talk to God every night and he just keeps whipping me and whipping me. It's like He is saying, I chose you to do my work and my Will, my Will be done in your life. I remember one night all I could do was say yes Lord yes Lord. I'm sorry for the mess that I made. Please give me another chance. Man, it hurts it hurts.

Tyrone: Come on y'all we need to pray for deliverance for this Pastor come pray. *(They all start praying. Pastor Mayceo falls on his knees crying and praying, Lights get dim in barbershop a male angel comes out and lifts pastor Mayceo up to his feet and says you have been broken you have been restored. The angel leaves lights come back up. They are shouting)*

Pastor Mayceo: Thank you, God. Thank you. I'm going to call my wife. *(He leaves)*

Tyrone: That prayer took a lot out of me. Come on we are closing shop to celebrate Pastor Mayceo newfound life.

Scene Seven

First Lady Lisa calls sis Lawanda ring ring!

First Lady Lisa: Hello, are you on your way? This is the night for our meeting.

Sis. Lawanda: Can I still bring Lawan over to your place?

First Lady Lisa: Girl yes. My boys will be glad to have him.

Sis. Lawanda: I'm at your door. I was on the way when you called. *(They walk in)*

Terrance: Sis. Lawanda what you doing here? You were the one who broke up this family.

First Lady Lisa: No son it was your dad and I, we did it. And you know God is a forgiving God. How many times has he forgiven you?

Terrance: Well, you right, mom. I'm sorry. *(He goes to his room)*

Markus: Who is this boy?

Sis Lawanda: It's my son Lawan, and he is nine.

Markus: Sis Lawanda, I didn't know you had a son. I always saw you by yourself. *(He paused for a moment)* Is his dad white?

First Lady Lisa: It doesn't matter what color his dad is, he is a lovely little man.

Markus: But mom she is dark, and he is light bright.

First Lady Lisa: Boy go to your room.

Markus: But mom can he come too? We can play my games.

First Lady Lisa: Is it all right, Sis Lawanda?

Sis. Lawanda: Yes, will he be, okay?

First Lady Lisa: Yes, come on we are going to be late for the meeting. *(They leave)*

Scene Eight

Pete and his wife are talking at the table.

Wife: Good morning honey. I've been doing some thinking about Davesha. She is not happy here with us and no matter how badly her family treated her she still loves them and wants to go home.

Pete: But you always said you wanted a daughter, now we have one. You want to give her back? She will not be treated well. We can give her whatever she wants. We can make her happy

Wife: No baby. I see the hurt in her eyes, and I feel her pain. I never told you but the people that raised me were not my biological parents they did the same thing to me that we are doing to her. I don't want her to hate me. I hated the parents that raised me because they took me from my biological parents. If I want anything for her, I want her to be happy. I thought that if we could give her anything she wanted and that would make her happy, but it didn't. So, can we please drop her off at the church?

Pete: Yes, baby if that will make you happy.

They call Davesha downstairs.

Pete: Davesha, you up?

Davesha: Yes sir, I'm up.

Pete: Come downstairs for a minute.

Davesha: Ok *(She walks in the room)*

Wife: Good morning baby, we have something we want to

tell you.

Wife looks at Pete.

Wife: Go ahead tell her.

Pete: We have decided to take you back to your family.

Davesha starts crying.

Davesha: Thank you, thank you, when can I leave?

Pete: My wife and I will drop you off at your dad's church Sunday morning. One thing, no police. We will drop you off and leave. No one must ever know about this or who we are.

Davesha: I won't tell, please just drop me off. *(They all leave)*

Scene Nine

Pastor Smith and two bad boys at the church.

Pastor Smith: Come on guys y'all acting like wimps. Lift that cross and bring it up the stairs, put it in the closet. Thank you, guys.

Bad Guy 1: Pastor, I have a confession to make. It has been bothering me since we did it.

Bad Guy 2: If you are talking about what I think you are, it has been bothering me too. Pastor about six months ago we did a bad thing. We robbed a preacher's kid and left him there for dead. But we never heard anything else from it, so we left it alone.

Bad Guy 1: We would like to say we're sorry and ask the preacher's kid for forgiveness.

Pastor Smith: Who was the kid?

Bad Guy 2: We think it's Pastor Mayceo's son Terrence.

Pastor Smith: My God, God is really doing a work in and for this family. God does answer prayers.

Bad Guy 1: Do you know where we can find him?

Pastor Smith: Yes, in church on Sunday morning.

Bad Guy 2: We will be there. Can you come by and pick us up?

Pastor Smith: Yes, see you Sunday morning. Be up and ready, I don't like being late to God's house. They all give each other dap and leave.

Scene Ten

First Lady Lisa, Lawanda, Sis. Tammy and sis. Kim with Doctor Sue at the table talking.

Doctor Sue: I see we have a new body here tonight. If I may ask what's your name?

Sis. Tammy: Hoe.

Doctor Sue: I'm not talking to you sis. Tammy, now let me ask you again what's your name?

Sis. Tammy: Sis. Hoe.

Sis. Lawanda: That's why I didn't want to come here. I knew everyone would judge me. I'm leaving.

Doctor Sue: Wait a minute, come here Sis. Tammy. *(Sis. Tammy gets up from the table and walks over to doctor sue)*

Doctor Sue: If you can't act like a lady, you are going to have to leave. Now what do you want?

Sis. Tammy: Well, she is a hoe. That's why we don't have a pastor at our church. She was doing the both of them.

Doctor Sue: This is a Christian center and if we can't help people get delivered from the things they are doing or have done then we are not doing God no good. It's people like you who keep people out of church. Now you're going to sit there and let her talk. Do you understand Sis?

Sis. Tammy: Yes ok. *(She waddles back to her seat)*

Doctor Sue: ok let's start over. Sis. What is your name?

Sis. Lawanda: Sis. Lawanda Hobart. *(Sis. Tammy laughs)*
Sis. Tammy told you she was a hoe.

Doctor Sue: One more remark out of you and you going to stand in the corner, this is a shame got to treat some grown people like children.

Sis. Lawanda: I'm not a hoe I just had some hang ups in life.

Doctor Sue: Like what?

Sis. Lawanda: I liked nice things and would do almost anything to get what I wanted. But then I got caught up in a game twice. One with a man that is Caucasian. He was the love of my life, and he didn't tell me he was married until three years later. By that time, I was 2 months pregnant with my son, Lawan. He is the best thing that ever happened to me. Then with pastor Mayceo and his family. I have messed up a lot of people's lives *(She starts crying)* I'm sorry I'm sorry. God, please help me please help me. They all pray for each other. *(Sis. Lawanda jumps up)* I'm going back to church. They all hug and leave.

Scene Eleven

Pastor Mayceo sitting in the chair looking at his phone wondering if he should call his wife.

First Lady Lisa calls Pastor Mayceo; Ring ring

Pastor Mayceo: Hello?

First Lady Lisa: Hello, how are you?

Pastor Mayceo: Is this my wife, baby? Why did we have to separate? We said we were going to stay together until we found our daughter.

First Lady Lisa: I couldn't stay with you after all that happened. You with Lawanda, me with Lawanda, our daughter missing. And still missing! I want you to know that I forgive you.

Pastor Mayceo: I know if I would have been home it would not have happened this way. I ran all the time forgetting about you and the children thinking you and the children was going to be there. Baby, I'm sorry. I want to know if I can come back home. God has done a work in my life. Just give me one more chance. *(Music)*

First Lady Lisa: I've been thinking the same thing. Can we try it again? God has forgiven the both of us. Now we need to forgive each other and move on.

Pastor Mayceo: *(Starts to cry)* Yes, baby yes.

First Lady Lisa: Okay, we can start it off by going back to church Sunday.

Pastor Mayceo: Yes, I think that will be great. I'll call Deacon Tom and Lee to let them know.

First Lady Lisa: I'll see you at church.

Pastor Mayceo: Will you bring the boys?

First Lady Lisa: Yes.

Pastor Mayceo: Ok. See you soon. *(They hang up)*

Pastor Mayceo: *(Calls Deacon Tom)* Hello, is this Deacon Tom?

Deacon Tom: Yes. Is this Pastor Mayceo?

Pastor Macao: Yes, it is. How you are?

Deacon Tom: I'm fine. It is good to hear from you. I thought you had dropped off the face of the earth. *(laughs)*

Pastor Mayceo: No, I'm still here. I would like to know if you have gotten someone to take my place at the church.

Deacon Tom: No pastor can't say we have.

Pastor Mayceo: God has done a change in my life, and I would like to know if I can take my place in the role of the Pastor again.

Deacon Tom: Well, you know pastor, we have not filled the role of pastor yet, and we have to take a vote on it. I would love to have you back as long as we can continue to look at those sexy ladies that come in the door with their nice donkudons. *(He laughs.)*

Pastor Mayceo: Well, you know I'm a changed man now Deacon. The only lady I have eyes for is my wife, Lisa.

Deacon Tom: You may have eyes for only your wife, but

my wife died a hundred years ago, so I can look all I want. Sorry for you changed man. God still needs to work in my life.

Pastor Mayceo: Oh, God will. If he can change me, I know he can change you.

Deacon Tom: The last person that tried to change me is 6 feet under, and she has been there for one hundred years, or it seems like one hundred years. I know what you are thinking that I killed her but no I didn't, she killed herself by always running after me.

Pastor Mayceo: Deacon that is too much information. I'll see you Sunday in church. (Hangs up, Pastor calls Deacon Lee.)

Pastor Mayceo: Hello?

Ladies voice: Hello.

Pastor Mayceo: Can I speak with Deacon Lee?

Ladies voice: Hold on (she calls for Deacon Lee.) Pick up the phone.

Deacon Lee: Hello?

Pastor Mayceo: Hello, Deacon Lee. I talked with deacon Tom and I asked him if I could come back and be the head pastor of the church again. I know I have had some shortcomings but I'm really ready now to take the call God has on my life and take it seriously.

Deacon Lee: Are you sure that's what you want to do? You had all the ladies chasing you.

Pastor Mayceo: Yes, I'm sure. Deacon Lee, well, God

gave me another chance so we can see what God has done in your life. If any I'll give it another try.

Pastor Mayceo: Good. Thank you, I'll see you in church Sunday. *(They hang up)*

\

Scene Twelve

First Lady and Sis. Lawanda back at the First Lady's house.

Sis. Lawanda: Thank you for inviting me out to the meeting today.

First Lady Lisa: You're welcome.

Sis. Lawanda: Look, I've been wondering if I should call Lawan's father.

First Lady Lisa: Why not? You need to make peace with his dad.

Sis. Lawanda: Can I make the call now; here with you? I think I really need some support on this one.

First lady Lisa: Yes, just tell him the truth.

Sis. Lawanda: The only number I have on him is his work number, should I call his job?

First Lady Lisa: What are you waiting for? I'm here for you. Call!

(Sis Lawanda picks up the phone and calls and man picks up.)

Lawyer: Hello?

Sis. Lawanda: Hello is Mr. Concord there?

Lawyer: Who wants to know?

Sis. Lawanda: I just need to talk with him if he's there.

Lawyer: Like I said, who wants to know?

Sis. Lawanda: This is a friend of his. Can I speak with him please?

Lawyer: What is the problem, I'm the closest thing you are going to get to him. So, tell me what's going on.

Sis. Lawanda: Are you sure I can talk to you? What do you think, First Lady?

First Lady Lisa: Yes, tell him.

Sis. Lawanda: Mr. Concord and I dated at one time, and I got pregnant and never told him. I know this is going to be hard for him to handle but I had to come clean. See, God had to work in me before I could even let anyone see my son. See, I'm black and he's white, so we didn't want to put it out in the open because of his status in life. I'm a nobody, and he is a powerful lawyer. But I need to tell him the truth that he has a son, and he is nine years old.

Lawyer: My God, My God, child. I'm a God-fearing man and no matter what the color of my grandson I will accept him. This is his father. I have some bad news to tell you, but he died two years ago in a motorcycle accident, he was our only son. He mentioned a lady and said her name was Lawanda and he loved her with all his heart, but she left him. You didn't know he had already gotten his divorce. He was only making sure you wanted him for him, not his money. But I have a grandson.

Sis. Lawanda: Yes sir.

Lawyer: I have some wonderful news for you, my dear. You and your son and my grandson will never want for anything. I've been holding on to this will for two years. You had one more year before it expired and everything, he left you would have been going to charity. God is truly in the midst of this. You won't have to work anymore, and your son will be taken care of for the rest of his life. He left you 9.9 billion dollars.

Sis. Lawanda: *(screams)* Oh my God! *(She cries and the boys run out)*

Lawan: What's wrong mommy, please don't cry.

Sis. Lawanda: You are just like your dad, kind, gentle and humble. He left his spirit with you. Baby we are rich, your dad left us all the money we need. Thank you, God, God really does answer prayers.

Lawyer: We will meet a little later, and we will discuss the details.

Sis. Lawanda: Ok, thank you so much. (They hang up)

All the boys start dancing and singing we rich we rich.

Sis. Lawanda: Ok boys, we don't have the money yet. Let's wait to celebrate after we get the money. (They all leave.)

Scene Thirteen

Sunday Morning, they all meet at the front of the church talking and laughing. They enter the church and see the pastor coming from the back office. They look at each other, silently in the church.

Pastor Mayceo: Good morning church, I know I have some explaining to do, but I want to tell you that I'm a changed man. God has delivered me from the mess that I was in. He has made me free. Thank God no more chains holding me. Hallelujah.

Sis: Tammy: I knew you was coming back (She turns around and looks at the other members.) I told you.

Dasha: Sis. Tammy, can we please hear what he has to say?

Sis. Kim: Girl, he's still fine. God sure did a work in you; you look brand new. Lord Jesus helped me.

Deacon: Tom. Can y'all let the pastor speak?

Deacon Lee: Yes please, I want to hear what he got to say.

(The door opens up. The pastor's wife and Sis. Lawanda walks in.)

Deacon Tom: *(Falls out of his seat)*

Deacon Lee: What in the hells heavens is going on here?

Sis. Tammy: *(Talking to Sis. Kim)* I wonder if they still doing each other.

Sis. Kim: I don't know, I don't know, let's hear what they got to say.

First Lady Lisa: I know this looks funny but it's nothing going on. God has done a great work in us. God has broken the chain of homosexuality over both of our lives.

Sis. Lawanda: And I have a son. His name is Lawan. Lawan come on in baby it's ok. God has made me free, no more chains holding me.

(Lawan comes in and holds onto his mommy.)

Sis. Lawanda: Baby you don't need to be afraid; God is working everything out for us.

Lawan: Ok, mom. *(He goes in the back and sits down)*

Terrance: Come on Markus, let's go and sit down.

Markus: Runs and hugs his dad before he sits down.

(The door opens, and it is the two bad guys with Pastor Smith.)

(Terrance jumps up to the guys who jumped him.)

Pastor Smith: Hold up, Terrance, they have something they want to say.

Bad Guy 1: Preacher boy, please will you forgive me? I'm sorry we could have killed you.

Bad Guy 2: If we can just learn to love each other it will be a better place. I'm so sorry, here are your shoes back.

Pastor Mayceo: Do you accept their apology, son?

(Terrance gets up and walks over to the guys, with a mad face.)

Terrance: Guys, I accept your apology. But I hope you really have changed your life because the next person you may just kill. God has given you another chance.

First Lady Lisa: I need now is for our daughter to come home. The church starts to pray for their daughter.

Everybody is praying, and Davesha walks through the door. *(Prayer stops)*

Deacon Lee: God really moved fast on this one.

Davesha: Dad, mommy I'm home. I'm home. (Dad and mommy crying.)

(Terrance and Markus run up to her and hug her)

Pastor Mayceo: My daughter is home. *(He falls on his knees crying and thanking God)*

Sis. Lawanda: What happened to the man that kidnapped you?

Davesha: They were good people, they wanted me to be their daughter, but I kept telling them that I wanted to go home.

Markus: Did they hurt you?

Davesha: No No! They gave me anything I wanted. Clothes, car, whatever I wanted, it was mine. All I had to do was ask.

Pastor Mayceo: Tell us who took you please baby.

Davesha: No, daddy they said no cops, and I gave them my word. They are really nice people, and they wanted me. You and mom are always gone, will we be a family again? *(Turns and looks at her mother then turns and looks at her father)* They both say yes at the same time.

Pastor Mayceo: Now let's get back to service. Will you have me again as your pastor? *(All the church raised their hands)*

Sis. Tammy: *(Gets up)* My work here is done. I told y'all

God was going to bring him back. Halleluiah! halleluiah! They all sing together as they walk off the stage.

The end